915.99 Lye, Keith
LYE
    Take a trip to
      Philippines

DATE			
APR 23 '87	13		
APR 30 '87	13		
MAY 11 '87	13		
MAY 14 '87	3		
MAY 21 '87			
JAN 21 '88	10		
OCT 2 '88	15		
	15		
JAN	15		

55529

PHILIPPINES

Keith Lye

General Editor

Henry Pluckrose

Franklin Watts

London   New York   Sydney   Toronto

Facts about The Philippines

Area:
300,000 sq. km.
(115,831 sq. miles)

Population:
51,950,000

Capital:
Manila

Largest Cities:
Manila (pop. with
  suburbs, 5,926,000)
Davao (610,000)
Cebu (490,000)

Official language:
Pilipino

Religions:
Christianity (Roman
Catholics 85 per cent;
Protestants 8 per cent)

Main exports:
Electronics, clothes, sugar,
coconut oil, copper
concentrates, gold,
bananas

Currency:
Philippine peso

Franklin Watts Limited
12a Golden Square
London W1

ISBN: UK Edition 0 86313 272 3
ISBN: US Edition 0 531 10013 8
Library of Congress Catalog
Card No: 85–50165

© Franklin Watts Limited 1985

Typeset by Ace Filmsetting Ltd,
Frome, Somerset
Printed in Hong Kong

Maps: Tony Payne
Design: Edward Kinsey
Stamps: Stanley Gibbons Limited
Photographs: Zefa; Paul Forrester, 8;
J. Allan Cash, 10, 14, 18, 19, 25;
Camerapix Hutchison, 11, 27, 31;
Robert Harding, 12, 28, 29
Front cover: Zefa
Back cover: Camerapix Hutchison

The Republic of the Philippines is an island country in southeast Asia. It is the same size as Italy, but it contains nearly 7,100 islands. Some are mountainous. Others are tiny coral islets. The picture shows the port of Tagbilaren on Bohol, the country's tenth largest island.

Nearly nine-tenths of the country's islands are uninhabited and three-fifths do not have names. Luzon is the largest island, making up one-third of the country. It has several volcanoes, including Mount Mayon, shown here.

Mindanao in the southeast is the country's second largest island. Many of its people are fishermen, who live in houses on stilts along the coast. They use small boats with bright sails, shown here at the village of Rio Hondo.

In mountainous areas, farmers
have cut steps, called terraces, into
the steep hillsides in order to grow
crops. Forests cover about two-fifths
of the Philippines, which has a hot
and wet tropical climate.

Manila is the capital, chief seaport and largest city. It is on the island of Luzon and was founded in 1571 by Spanish settlers. As in many other large cities, its streets are often blocked by traffic jams.

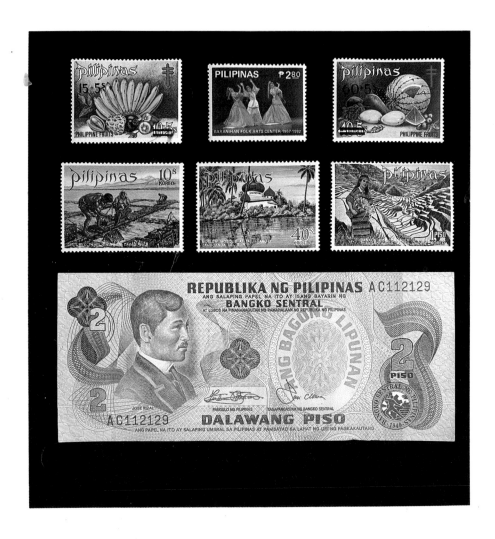

The picture shows some stamps
and money used in the Philippines.
The main unit of currency is the peso,
which contains 100 centavos.

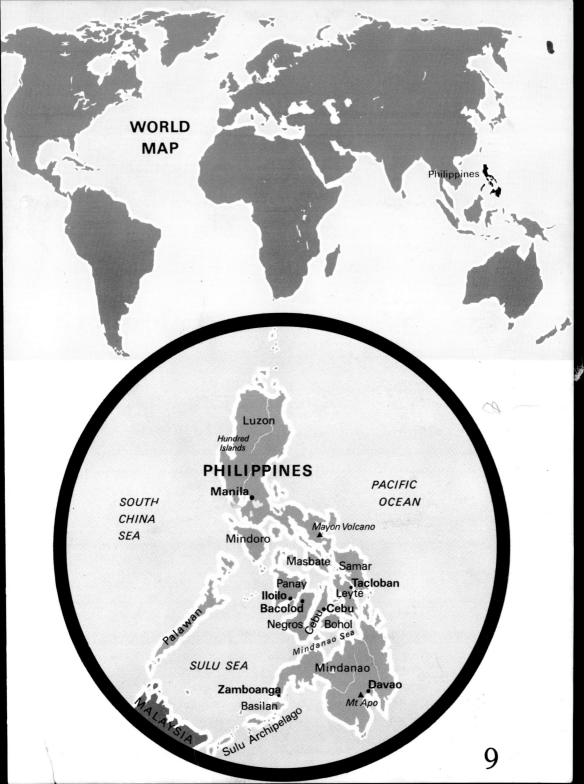

WORLD
MAP

Philippines

Luzon

Hundred
Islands

PHILIPPINES

SOUTH
CHINA
SEA

Manila

PACIFIC
OCEAN

Mayon Volcano

Mindoro

Masbate

Samar

Panay

Tacloban

Iloilo

Leyte

Bacolod

Cebu

Cebu

Negros

Bohol

Palawan

Mindanao Sea

SULU SEA

Mindanao

Zamboanga

Davao

Basilan

Mt Apo

MALAYSIA

Sulu Archipelago

9

The Head of State in the Philippines lives in the President's Palace in Manila. The President usually governs with an elected National Assembly. But in recent years, rivalries between Muslims (called Moros) and Christians, and Communist uprisings have caused many problems for the government.

The people of the Philippines are called Filipinos. Most of them are of Malay origin, because their ancestors came from the mainland of Southeast Asia. There are also some people of Chinese and European descent, together with Negritos (pygmies) and some tribal groups in remote areas.

11

The people in country areas, as
here in northern Luzon, are poorer
than the people in the cities. Many of
them live in one-roomed, thatched
houses. Their main food is rice, seen
growing here in the field below the
path.

12

Northern Luzon contains the world's largest terraces for rice growing. They were built by a group of hill people, the Ifugao. These Ifugao elders are wearing ceremonial costumes. Many still follow local religions.

The Portuguese navigator
Ferdinand Magellan, who led a
Spanish expedition, introduced
Christianity in 1521. Bits of his cross
are inside this black cross kept in
Cebu City, on Cebu Island, where he
landed. The paintings show the
conversion of the Filipinos.

This church in Luzon is one of many Spanish-built Roman Catholic churches in the Philippines. The Spanish ruled the country from 1565. They named it after their king, Philip II. In 1898, after the Spanish-American War, the United States took over the islands.

About four per cent of the people in the Philippines are Muslims. Many Muslim fishermen live in coastal villages on Mindanao. Others live on the small islands that make up the Sulu Archipelago (group of islands).

The Chinese have traded with the Philippines since early times. A sizeable Chinese community lives on the island of Cebu, where this Taoist temple stands. Taoism is an ancient Chinese religion.

In December 1941, Japan attacked the Philippines. Filipino and American troops fought bravely. The picture shows two of their guns at Corregidor, a small island at the mouth of Manila Bay, Luzon. But the Philippines surrendered in April and May 1942.

These statues show the American General Douglas MacArthur leading troops ashore in October 1944. From their first landing here on Red Beach, on Leyte Island, those troops liberated the country. In 1946, the Philippines achieved full independence.

About 46 out of every 100 people
work on farms, as compared with 17
in industry. Nearly half the land is
farmed. The chief crops are rice, seen
growing here in terraces on Luzon,
abaca (or Manila hemp), copra,
sugar cane, maize and tobacco.

The Philippines is one of the world's top ten rice producers. Rice is the leading crop in the country and most Filipinos eat rice with nearly every meal. Here, freshly gathered stalks are laid out to dry.

This Filipino girl is hanging up
fresh tobacco leaves to dry. Most of
the tobacco is processed in local
factories. By making its own cigars
and cigarettes, the country saves
money on its import bills.

Animal farming is important. The country has about 2.8 million carabaos (water buffaloes), which are used as beasts of burden. There are also 1.9 million cattle, 7.8 million pigs, 1.6 million goats and 58 million poultry.

The Philippines has a variety of industries and manufactured goods now top the country's exports. Traditional crafts, such as making carpets from abaca, also flourish. The steady increase in industry in recent years has made the country more prosperous.

Fishing is important. Most of the catch comes from sea-fishing, but more than an eighth of the fish eaten in the country are raised in ponds. This fishing village is in Cebu.

About a quarter of adults in the
Philippines cannot read or write.
Comic books are very popular
reading material. The picture shows
a lending library for comics in Manila.

Elementary, or primary, education is free and compulsory for six years. Most secondary schools are private and two-thirds of children of secondary school age attend school.

People in country areas often build their homes with bamboo poles. The houses are raised above ground level to prevent dampness. Cooking is usually done on open fires.

The Filipinos grow many fruits, including bananas, breadfruit, mangoes, papayas and pineapples. Fresh bananas and pineapples canned in syrup are exported from the Philippines.

The Philippines attracts many tourists with its beautiful scenery and beaches, such as here at Puerto Galena on Mindoro island. Nearly 900,000 visitors arrived in 1982. Tourism is now a major industry.

The Filipinos have many religious
festivals. In January, the Roman
Catholics of Quiapo, a district in
Manila, carry a heavy cross through
the streets to celebrate the Festival
of the Black Nazarene.

Index